A Great Idea

The Seed Vault

by Bonnie Juettner

NORWOOD HOUSE PRESS

Norwood House Press
P.O. Box 316598
Chicago, Illinois 60631

For information regarding Norwood House Press, please visit our Web site at:

www.norwoodhousepress.com or call 866-565-2900.

PHOTO CREDITS: Cover: Launette Florian/Maxppp/Landov; © AFP/Getty Images, 29; AP Images, 5, 7, 11, 12, 14, 22, 25, 27, 30, 32, 36; © Agripicture Images/Alamy, 4; © AKG/Johann Brandstetter, 8, 17; Eliyahu Ben Yigal/Israel Sun/Landov, 10; Enrique Castro-Mendivil/Reuters/Landov, 9; © Getty Images, 39; © Gianni Dagli Ortiz/Corbis, 16; © Global Crop Diversity/epa/Corbis, 31; © Jim Richardson Corbis, 42; © Nigel Cattlin/Alamy, 13; © RIA Novosti/Alamy, 19, 20; © Radu Sigheti/Corbis, 35; Reuters/Landov, 33; © Robert Bird/Alamy, 24

LIBRARY OF CONGRESS CATALOGING-IN-PUBLICATION DATA

Juettner, Bonnie.
  The seed vault / Bonnie Juettner.
    p. cm. — (A great idea)
  Summary: "The seed vault in Norway houses plant seeds from around the world to be stored in the event that the plant needs to be re-introduced into the food supply"—Provided by publisher.
  Includes bibliographical references and index.
  ISBN-13: 978-1-59953-343-8 (library edition : alk. paper)
  ISBN-10: 1-59953-343-X (library edition : alk. paper)
1. Gene banks, Plant—Juvenile literature. 2. Seeds—Storage—Juvenile literature. I. Title. II. Series: Great idea.
  SB123.3.J84 2009
  631.5'21—dc22
                                                      2009016567

Manufactured in the United States of America.

Contents

Note: Words that are **bolded** in the text are defined in the glossary on page 44.

Chapter 1

Keeping Our Food Safe

Oxeye daisies growing wild alongside planted barley (left) is an excellent example of plant diversity. Numerous species of plants coexist throughout the world.

Scientists think that in 100 years, half of the world's species may be **extinct**. When people think of a species becoming extinct, they often think of animal species that are endangered. But plant species are being lost as well.

Scientists worry about losing plant diversity— the many different species of plants that exist. They worry for two reasons. First, more than half of prescription drugs come from chemicals that are made by plants. Scientists have not analyzed all the world's plants yet. Somewhere, there might be a plant that makes a chemical that could be used to fight cancer, diabetes, or heart disease. Or there might be a plant that makes a chemical that helps people to recover from infections. Whenever a plant becomes extinct from disease or human interaction, scientists lose any hope that a medicine could have been made from that plant.

Perhaps more importantly though, many plants are used as food. Every plant that

Plant Diseases

Just like humans, plants can get sick. Plant diseases, like human diseases, are caused by bacteria, viruses, and fungi. Plant diseases are usually named after what they do to the plant. A blight usually means that the whole plant, or an important part of it, has died. Some plant diseases do not affect the whole plant.

Plant diseases spread faster when plants are grown as crops. In the wild, plants of the same species may grow far from each other. When farmers plant crops in fields, however, the plants grow side by side. This makes it easier for a disease to spread from one plant to another.

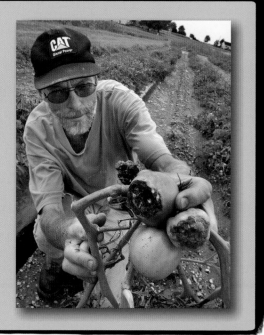

Sickly tomatoes show the deadly effects of blight, which can spread rapidly throughout plants.

exists is uniquely adapted to its environment. It is possible that some plants might be uniquely adapted to survive in parts of the world that are experiencing climate change. Some parts of China, for example, are experiencing droughts as the climate gets dryer. Somewhere, there might be a food **crop** that is perfectly adapted to grow in dry weather. Other parts of the world are experiencing more floods than they used to. Somewhere, there might be plants that are adapted to seasonal flooding. If these plants become extinct, they cannot help feed people in the areas that flood.

Centers of Crop Diversity

Some parts of the world have many different types of the same crop that grow side by side. Those areas act like centers for those types of plants. The Andes Mountains in South America are an example. The mountains are home to thousands of kinds of potatoes. That makes them a center for the potato. Central America is a center for corn. The Oaxaca, Mexico region alone, for example, has 85,000 unique varieties of corn. Each variety is a little different from the others. Some varieties of corn are small; others are large. Some have yellow kernels, while others have red or blue kernels.

A farmer shows two different types of corn in Oaxaca, Mexico. The area has thousands of corn varieties that adapt to different weather conditions.

Scientists consider every center of crop diversity to be a treasure. Farmers know from experience that crossing different varieties of crops together can produce a new **variation** that is even hardier, or stronger, than the ones that came before. The new crop might be able to live through conditions that would kill other varieties. A hardy crop might live through a flood that would kill other plants. Or it might be less attractive to insects. New crop variations could also be used in place of a less productive crop. The new variation might be able to produce more food to feed more people. Different strains of a crop also make protection from plant diseases possible. A plant disease may attack one strain of a crop. Farmers can then plant a different strain—one that is similar, but resists disease.

Adapting to Changing Temperatures

One challenge that faces modern farmers is climate change. In many places, the weather is changing. The weather is getting warmer in some places. It is getting dryer or wetter in others. Vicente Hermogenes Baca Huaman is a potato farmer in Peru. His ancestors have farmed in the Andes Mountains for centuries. They crossed different varieties of potatoes together to produce several plants that were perfectly adapted for these cold mountains. Temperatures there average 53 degrees Fahrenheit (12 degrees Celsius). For several years now, though, Baca Huaman has had to plant his potatoes higher up the mountain than his ancestors did. The fields lower down the mountain are not cold enough to keep the potatoes healthy. It takes him about an

Quechuan Indians harvest potatoes in Peru. Farmers have grown potatoes in the Andes Mountains for centuries.

A farmer digs up potatoes that are native to his home in the highlands of the Andes. Climate changes in the mountain range affect potato crops.

hour and 20 minutes to climb to his potato field from his home.

Baca Huaman recalled in a 2009 National Public Radio interview, "When I was a boy, I used to go with my father to the mountain and it would be covered in snow. We would see snow all over these fields. There is never snow here anymore." The climate in the Andes is changing. The weather is warmer, most of the time. But sometimes there is a sudden freeze. The odd weather can cause the potatoes to catch a fungus called late **blight**. (Late blight is just one type of blight. It is a type of blight that affects potatoes. There are other blights that affect different plants.)

? Did You Know?

Some plants, such as peas, live only one year. Farmers have to replant these crops every year or two. Many others, such as beets, carrots, and parsley, live for two or more years.

Fighting Plant Diseases

Seed banks provide farmers with one way to fight disease. They can get new seeds. Then they can plant a species that is similar but not exactly the same as the old one. The new species may be better at resisting disease.

Plant diseases can be fought in other ways, too. Farmers can spray the plants with chemicals that kill bacteria or viruses or that keep insects away. They can also rotate their crops. Rotating means that farmers can plant one crop one year and a different crop the next year. Sometimes farmers even burn their fields to get rid of a disease.

A common method of fighting plant disease is crop dusting. Here an airplane sprays pesticide over potato fields in Israel.

Coping with the weather is not new to Andean potato farmers, however. They protect themselves by growing many different crops. They grow corn and quinoa (a type of grain). They also grow many other kinds of potatoes. Thousands of different types of potatoes grow there. Each village has a potato collection, and the collections may include a few hundred types of potatoes. The potato plays an important part in Andean culture. One kind of potato is eaten after a boy has his first haircut, for example. A bumpy, grape-size potato must be peeled by a man's bride-to-be. She does this to prove to the man's parents that she will be dedicated to her new family.

A Potato Bank

Andean farmers do not grow so many kinds of potatoes just for fun. They have good reasons. Each potato has different **genes**. Genes carry a plant's DNA. DNA is the blueprint that tells the plant how to grow and develop. Different genes make some potatoes grow better in dark, moist conditions. Others grow better in the sun. Some potatoes are better at resisting blight. Farmers in the Andes pay close attention to the weather. They try to plant the types of potatoes that will grow best in the season they expect. Or they do as Baca Huaman does. They move their crops to a location that will improve their chances. Farmers do what they have to do to ensure they will have food to eat.

A crop from Peru reflects the extraordinary genetic diversity of potatoes grown in the mountainous region.

Scientists in Peru are trying to do what Andean farmers do, but on a larger scale. The International Potato Center is located in Lima, Peru. The Potato Center has potatoes in every stage of the plant's development. Farmers can go there to get seeds or seedlings (plants that have just started to grow). They can also get fully grown potatoes. The Potato Center also stores sweet potatoes and root vegetables. Most importantly, though, it stores hundreds of different gene types for each plant. It is a potato gene bank.

Food Security

Plant gene banks like the International Potato Center help protect the food supply. Just like humans, plants can get diseases. They are also at risk from insects.

Bad weather, such as droughts and floods, can also destroy a food crop. When these things happen, **famine** can be the result.

Famine brings disastrous consequences to every animal in the food chain. Here a cow suffering from malnutrition searches for food.

A famine is more likely to occur after a plant disease outbreak or a flood if a community has been depending on just one type of plant for its food supply. The food supply is safer when nations rely on many different varieties of plants for food. A disease that kills one type of plant may leave others untouched. Some plants can survive after living in flooded fields for two weeks—others cannot. For centuries, farmers have crossed different varieties of plants together. They try to breed plants that are hardier. These plants can survive even if weather conditions change suddenly. And the farmers have saved seeds from many different varieties of plants. Then they have the option of planting other strains when conditions change.

What Is a Seed?

A seed is the embryo, or fertilized egg, of a plant. Stored around each embryo is a layer of food to nourish it. Around that is a coating that protects the seed until it is time to sprout.

Seeds begin to sprout, or **germinate**, when there is enough warmth and moisture around them. That is why seeds in the wild sprout in springtime, because that is when the weather gets warmer. To save seeds, farmers stop them from sprouting by keeping them cool and dry. Seeds may be kept for many years this way. They will not last forever, though.

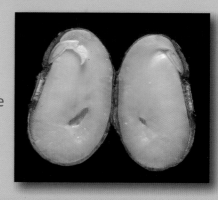

Cut in two, the protective coating of a runner bean seed can be seen.

Food research scientists sort through many varieties of rice from Thailand. The rice grains will be stored in a seed bank for future use.

Plant diversity is threatened in our world today. The climate is changing. It is becoming warmer in some places and moister or dryer in others. Many plants have been lost as cities and towns expand, mines are dug, or forests are cut down. Many scientists think that two-thirds of the world's wild plant species may be extinct by the year 2100. To combat this, scientists wanted to form a new bank that will keep seeds from all over the world. This bank could be used by farmers everywhere to help them grow plants that are the best for their areas.

Chapter 2

Seed Banks in History

Archaeologists are scientists who study remains of past civilizations. They have found the remains of what they believe are some of the world's first farms in several places around the world. In Iraq, archaeologists found farms dating from about 6750 B.C. The archaeologists study items found on these farms. Their studies help them understand how ancient farmers grew their crops.

Archaeologists learned that farmers always did two things at the end of the growing season. They harvested the crops for food. And they also set aside some of the seeds to plant the following year. Archaeologists know this because they found some of the seeds that had been saved. To save the seeds, farmers had to put them in a secure location. They could have been destroyed by weather that was too cold or too hot. They could also have been destroyed by floods. Also, birds and other animals like to eat seeds. Farmers had to keep their seeds safe from hungry animals.

Ancient Seed Savers

Archaeologists think that ancient Iraqi farmers looked carefully at their wheat crops. The farmers took the healthiest plants and saved some of their kernels. Then they decided how best to keep the seeds safe. Some farmers decided to bury them. Archaeologists know that the first farmers were women. These farmers used things they had in their homes to save seeds in. They wove baskets and filled

them with cold ashes. Then they nestled the seeds carefully into the middle of the ashes in the baskets. The ashes would keep the seeds cool. They would also disguise their smell, so animals could not find them.

Archaeologists discovered this ancient container that kept precious seeds safe from one growing season to the next.

The farmers buried the baskets in places where they could find them again. Some seed baskets were not found again by the farmers, however. Instead, archaeologists found them thousands of years later.

The farmers did the same thing again and again with other batches of seeds. Saving several batches probably made early farmers feel much safer. They hoped at least one batch would survive the winter. If a farmer's family moved, she could dig up the seed baskets. She could take them with her and rebury them in a new location.

This drawing shows a Stone Age hut with different types of stockpiling jars and baskets used for storing seeds.

Not all farmers buried seeds in ash-filled baskets. Farmers in different parts of the world used different materials. They used the materials they had nearby that helped protect the seeds from what could harm or eat them. Some farmers in the Americas made seed containers out of clay. Then they made straw huts on poles high above the ground. They put the clay seed containers in the huts. That kept the seeds safe from animals and floods.

Not all ancient farmers saved seeds from exactly the same plants. In ancient times, many varieties of plants such as wheat and millet grew in the wild. In each place the plants were slightly different. Different farmers in the same area might save seeds from different varieties of wheat and millet. This enabled thou-

sands of varieties of crops to be saved for future farmers to plant.

Vavilov's Seed Bank

Most ancient farmers saved only enough seeds to plant their own crops. It was not until thousands of years later that a scientist decided to start a world seed bank. The first scientist to try it was Nikolai Vavilov. He was a Russian biologist and plant breeder.

Vavilov lived in the early twentieth century. He had been studying genes and DNA. At the time, genetics was a new science. Vavilov realized that plant breeding could become a science, too. All that plant breeders needed was a wide variety of plants and seeds to work with. Vavilov began collecting and making lists of ancient and wild varieties of crops. He traveled throughout the world collecting wheat, barley, lentils, and many other crops.

Nikolai Vavilov

Nikolai Vavilov lived during a time of war. He lived through the Russian Revolution, World War I, and World War II. But the wars did not stop Vavilov from traveling. He went on more than 100 trips to other countries. Vavilov traveled throughout Asia. He also visited North and South America and Africa. He hoped to cross different plant breeds together. He wanted to breed hardy plants that could survive early frosts. He wanted to breed plants that would produce more food.

During his travels, Vavilov noticed that crops are scattered unevenly around the world. Some places have more varieties of crops than others. He made a map that showed eight centers of crop diversity. Vavilov was one of the first scientists to make such a map.

Nikolai Vavilov looks over a map he created of various centers of plant diversity around the world.

Vavilov also convinced his students to collect seeds with him. He put together teams of students to collect them. Over 20 years, Vavilov collected 60,000 wild seed samples from 64 countries. Together, the teams collected 250,000 seed samples.

Unfortunately, Vavilov lived in difficult times. He lived through the Russian Revolution, when Russia became a Communist country. Russia became part of the Soviet Union, a country which no longer exists today. The Soviet Union included Russia, Ukraine, Belarus, Latvia, Lithuania, Estonia, Armenia, Georgia, Azerbaijan, Kazakhstan, and other countries. These countries are independent today. During World War II, the Soviet Union was ruled by Joseph Stalin, a dictator. People living in Stalin's Russia did not have the freedom

Vavilov was honored by the Communist government with this memorial plaque at a plant research institute in Russia.

to say what they thought. Scientists did not have the freedom to study anything they chose. Vavilov was arrested for his work.

Vavilov was charged with treason and spying. It may be that his many trips to other countries led Soviet police to think he was a spy. Soviet police tortured Vavilov in prison. They forced him to confess that he was a spy, although he was not. He was tried in court and sentenced to be executed by a firing squad. Later though, Vavilov's sentence was reduced. Instead of being executed, he was sent to prison for 20 years.

Vavilov's students continued to work on the seed bank, but it was located in the city of Leningrad in the Soviet Union. During World War II, the Germans invaded the Soviet Union. They blockaded Leningrad so no food could get in

Did You Know?

Scientists do not know how many plant species there are in the world. At present, more than 260,000 plant species have been found.

or out of the city. Many people starved. Vavilov's students were with the seeds in the seed bank. Many seeds, such as kernels of corn and grains of rice, can be used as food. But Vavilov's students refused to eat the seeds. Instead, they fought to protect the seed bank. They fought off hungry mobs during the day. At night, they fought off packs of hungry rats. Several of the scientists starved

The World's Rice Bank

The International Rice Research Institute (IRRI) is the world's largest rice bank. It is also the oldest. But the IRRI does much more than just collect different varieties of rice. Scientists at the IRRI study rice. They are trying to find out how global warming may affect rice crops around the world. They also teach farmers how to take better care of their crops. They can help farmers fight insect pests and give them seeds to start a small crop.

The IRRI also breeds new varieties of rice. In 2009 it released a kind of rice that can survive a flood. Rice thrives in wet weather. But most rice will die if it is totally covered in water for more than four days. The IRRI's new rice is called Swarna Sub-1. It can survive in a flooded field for up to 17 days.

Laborers plant rice seedlings in experimental plots at the IRRI in the Philippines.

to death, surrounded by food. But they accomplished their goal. They saved the seed bank. Vavilov's seed bank still exists today. Today, it is called the Vavilov Institute. The Vavilov Institute inspired scientists in other countries to start seed banks of their own.

National Seed Banks

Since Vavilov's time, many nations have started their own seed banks. An international wheat and barley bank is located in Aleppo, Syria. The Philippines has the world's largest rice bank. The largest corn bank is in Mexico City, Mexico.

Nonfood plants, such as wildflowers and trees, also have seed banks. The New England Wildflower Society runs a bank of North American wildflower seeds. It

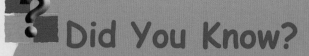

Did You Know?

Plants have adapted to live in very extreme conditions. Some live in parts of the world where the temperature never rises above freezing. Others live in deserts where the temperature is often over 100 degrees Fahrenheit (38 degrees Celsius).

concentrates on seeds from the northeastern United States. Other seed-saving groups run seed banks in other parts of the United States. Great Britain also has a seed bank. It works to save seeds from all the native plants of Great Britain. Many nations have their own seed banks. But some scientists believed that a world seed bank was needed.

Chapter 3

The "Doomsday" Seed Vault

The Millennium Seed Bank in England protects thousands of plant species found around the globe.

About 1,400 seed banks exist in the world today. Seeds in seed banks, though, may still be in danger. Many seed banks do not have long-term storage. They cannot keep seeds cool enough to last for very many years. "We think that fifty percent of the unique collections . . . are in danger," says Cary Fowler in the *Atlantic Monthly* magazine in 2007. Fowler works to collect and save seeds from around the

Storing Seeds in Banks

When seeds arrive at a seed bank, scientists sort, label, wash, and dry them. They dry the seeds enough to get the seeds' humidity level down to about 5 percent. Then they put the seeds in a cold room. Most seeds are kept at temperatures between 14 to –4 degrees Fahrenheit (–10 and –20 degrees Celsius). This is colder than the temperatures at which farmers save seeds. Farmers and **plant breeders** usually store seeds at room temperature, or a little cooler. But farmers and plant breeders only need their seeds to last for a few years. Seed banks want to keep their seeds for much longer. At very cold temperatures, seeds can last for more than 100 years. Many can even last for thousands of years.

Row upon row of seed jars are protected in this refrigerated vault outside Mexico City. The vault contains over 160,000 samples of wheat seeds and 25,000 samples of corn seeds.

To make sure that the seeds are still good, scientists germinate a few seeds from each sample every few years. If scientists cannot get enough seeds from a sample to germinate, they collect more.

world. "That's pretty stunning, when you think about it. As one scientist said to me, 'We call them seed banks, but actually they're more like morgues.'"

Danger to Seed Banks

Getting too warm is one danger that seeds in seed banks face. But seed banks are also at risk from natural disasters. In 1971 an earthquake destroyed Nicaragua's seed bank. In 1985 a starving group of people broke into a Peruvian seed bank. They took and ate its sweet potato collection. Honduras's seed bank was destroyed by Hurricane Mitch in 1998. In 2006 a Philippine seed bank was flooded during a typhoon. Sweet potato, taro, and banana seeds were washed away in a river of mud.

Did You Know?

Some seeds are so tiny that 2,500 could fit in a pod the size of your thumb. Others are big and heavy, and weigh more than a bowling ball, like the seed of a double coconut tree.

Wars can also threaten seed banks. In 2001 terrorists attacked the World Trade Center in New York City. In response, the United States went to war in Afghanistan. Afghanistan had been through war before. It only had one seed bank left. That seed bank was located in Kabul, the nation's capital city. Scientists there tried to protect the seeds from the war. They took the seeds out of Kabul, to the towns of Ghazni and

Restoring the American Chestnut

The year 1904 was the beginning of the end of the American chestnut tree. That year, a fungus arrived in North America from Asia. The fungus attacked chestnut and oak trees, but North American chestnuts were hit especially hard. By 1925 the fungus had spread over 1,000 miles (1,609km). Not all fungi are able to kill a whole tree, but the chestnut blight did. However, it did not kill every species it infected. It did not kill oak trees.

The fungus that caused the blight is still in North America. It lives in the bark of trees. Ever since the chestnut blight began, plant breeders have been trying to breed a new kind of chestnut tree. They used seeds from different varieties of chestnut. With the seeds, they hoped to produce a chestnut that could resist the fungus. In 2002 breeders at the American Chestnut Foundation began planting a chestnut tree that is 1/16th Asian chestnut and 15/16ths American chestnut. In 2005 breeders harvested the first chestnuts from the new trees. Soon the foundation hopes to start replanting the lost chestnut forests of the United States.

A volunteer tends an American chestnut tree at a breeding farm at Purdue University in Indiana. Several such programs hope to repopulate the country with chestnuts.

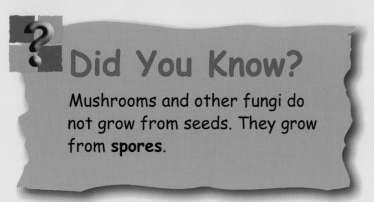

Jalalabad. They put the seeds in jars and hid them in the basements of two houses. Then the scientists fled the country. When they returned, they found that looters had dumped out the seeds. The looters wanted the jars that the seeds were in. Hundreds of unique Afghan seeds were destroyed. The seed bank had included rare varieties of almonds, walnuts, grapes, melons, cherries, plums, apricots, peaches, and pears.

During the war in Iraq, its national seed bank, located at Abu Ghraib, was destroyed. It had contained samples of ancient wheat, lentils, and chickpeas. Fortunately, many of the seed samples from Abu Ghraib were saved. Iraqi scientists knew that the country would soon be at war. They shipped as many seeds as they could to the seed bank in Aleppo, Syria.

A Back-Up Copy

For many years, scientists have tried to talk the world's leaders into saving more seeds. Many scientists were worried about how easily seed banks can be destroyed, flooded, or looted. They wanted a seed bank that could back up the other seed banks—the same way that a computer can back up files by making copies. In 2004 many of the

world's leaders signed a treaty. They agreed to try to preserve as many plant species as they could. The treaty also said they would support a world seed bank. Leaders of more than 100 nations signed this treaty.

A world seed bank, though, would have to be very secure. If it were destroyed, the world's seed collection would be destroyed. Scientists decided to make a seed bank so secure that it could be called a vault. They nicknamed the new vault the Doomsday Vault, because it can survive even a global disaster. It can survive wars and acts of terrorism. It can survive natural disasters. It can survive if its cooling systems fail. It can even survive a nuclear bomb.

An Arctic Vault

The Doomsday Vault is located in Norway, deep in the Arctic. Norway donated the land for the vault. It also paid for the cost of building it. To build it, engineers tunneled 400 feet (120m) into a mountain. Tunneling into the mountain was hard. The ground is permanently frozen. It is called permafrost. The seed vault has a refrigeration system to keep it cool. But even if the cooling system fails, the temperature inside the vault will not rise above

The Doomsday Vault under construction in Norway. The vault protects the world's diverse plant seeds in the event of global catastrophe.

freezing. The permafrost in which it sits is frozen all year round. Scientists imagined what would happen if the cooling system broke down. "Even if you waited a couple of years for the serviceman to show up," joked Geoffrey Hawtin in the *Washington Post* in 2006, "it won't really matter."

The mountain is also on high ground. It is 425 feet (130m) above sea level. Scientists say that the Doomsday Vault is so high up that it will never flood. Even if global warming caused all of Antarctica's ice to melt, the vault would still be above sea level.

The seed vault is also protected against attack by terrorists. To get into the vault, one has to pass through fences and several sets of steel doors. A video camera

An artist's rendering of the Doomsday Vault shows the finished vault drilled into a mountain cooled by permafrost. The vault will protect seeds from threats such as war or global warming.

An armed guard stands in front of the Doomsday Vault's entrance.

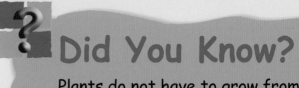

Did You Know?

Plants do not have to grow from seeds. They can also grow from cuttings from a grown plant. To get a cutting, gardeners cut a piece from an existing plant. The piece that is cut off is called the cutting. Gardeners place the cutting in water or damp soil. Potatoes are often grown this way.

takes pictures of everyone who passes through the tunnel. Motion detectors record every movement. Even to get to the tunnel, an intruder would have to pass through Norway's Arctic landscape. The area around the vault is home to many polar bears. Scientists believe the polar bears should help to discourage anyone who might consider trying to break into the seed vault.

The Doomsday Seed Collection

The Doomsday Vault is intended to hold samples of every possible kind of seed. Each batch of seeds will be stored in aluminum foil. There will be 500 seeds per batch. If each seed is about the size of a wheat seed, the vault has room for three million batches. That would equal about two billion seeds. The vault does not have that many seeds yet, however.

When the vault opened in 2008, more than 100 nations gave it seed samples. On the first day, about 100 million seeds were placed in the vault. The seeds came from 268,000 different kinds of plants. Each sample came from a different farm around the world and from every continent. Most seeds were from food crops, such as corn, rice, wheat, eggplant, lettuce, barley, and potato. Cary Fowler, who became the director of the seed vault, was pleased. "At these temperatures," he said in a 2008 interview with CNN, "seeds for important

At the seed vault, Kenyan Nobel Peace Prize laureate Wangan Maathai (left) and Norway's prime minister Jens Stoltenberg demonstrate the spirit of global cooperation.

Laws Against Saving Seeds

Sometimes, it is illegal to save seeds. Some seeds did not develop in nature. Instead, they were created by scientists working for large corporations. These seeds are still ordinary seeds. Like other seeds, they contain DNA—the genetic code that tells a plant's embryo how to grow and develop. Unlike an ordinary seed, though, the DNA in a seed created by a large corporation is patentable. A patent protects a person's unique idea from being copied. If someone wants to use the idea, he or she must get permission from the owner of the patent. The company that made the seeds requires farmers who buy the seeds to sign a contract. The contract says that the farmers agree not to save any seeds for the following year. Instead, they have to buy them again the next season.

In India, a group of women farmers decided to rebel against that. They refused to buy seeds from large corporations that won't let them save their seeds. Instead, they are saving India's native seeds. "Saving seeds is our duty," explains Vandana Shiva in a lecture in 2004. Shiva is the leader of a seed-saving group. "The women of India have evolved two hundred thousand rice varieties," says Shiva. "At no point did any one of those women turn around and tell her sister, 'Now I have bred this new rice . . . it is my property; now . . . you will pay me.'"

crops like wheat, barley, and peas can last for up to 10,000 years."

In 2009, a year after the seed vault opened, the world's nations decided to celebrate its birthday by sending more seeds. They sent 32 more kinds of potato, and 3,800 more varieties of wheat and barley. Most of these seeds were sent by national seed banks and international seed bank networks. But many were sent by seed collectors. These collectors, like Vavilov and his students, travel around the world. They search for different kinds of plants. When they find new species, they save the seeds. They package the seeds carefully and send them to the Doomsday Vault.

Chapter 4

Saving Rare Plants

Luigi Guarino is visiting an open-air market in Addis Ababa, Ethiopia. Ethiopia is in eastern Africa. It can be a dangerous area to visit.

Guarino, though, is there on a mission. He is looking for seeds. At the moment, he is looking specifically for beans. He hopes to find beans that can resist drought. A drought is caused by too little rainfall. It becomes too dry for most plants to grow.

Ethiopian women offer seeds for sale in an open-air market. Scientists are working to save unique seeds in the area in case of war.

Saving Nonfood Seeds

The Doomsday Vault is intended to preserve thousands of varieties of the world's food crops. But there are also seed banks dedicated to preserving plants that people do not eat, such as wildflowers and trees. The Millennium Seed Bank in Great Britain is one such seed bank. Scientists there hope to save samples of all of Great Britain's plants. The Millennium Seed Bank is also linked to similar seed banks around the world.

It is not obvious to everyone why seeds that do not produce food plants are important enough to save. Scientists know that it is important to save all seeds. They think that any plant may have genes that are important. Some plants are worth preserving just because they are part of Earth's natural history. Others may contain sub-

Paul Smith, director of the Millennium Seed Vault in England, explains heirloom seed origins of some of the plants there.

stances that could be used as medicines. Someday, the medicines that come from those plants could save people's lives.

The conflict between Ethiopia and neighboring Eritrea is another reason he is here. He hopes to save whatever unique seeds he can in case war breaks out. If there is war in this region, plants, as well as people, may be at risk. Fields might be burned or neglected. Some of Ethiopia's unique plant heritage could be lost forever.

Guarino's friend, Belgian scientist Daniel Debouck, also travels to dangerous parts of the world. He has spent 30 years exploring South American countries, especially Colombia. He travels through areas where a terrorist group operates. The terrorist group looks for foreigners to kidnap and hold as **hostages**. But Debouck believes that his work is important and that he needs to be there. Like Guarino, Debouck looks for unique beans to save. "He's married to the bean," jokes Guarino in *Popular Science* in 2008.

The Seed Collectors

Often seed collectors feel like secret agents. They travel to parts of the world that many people would never think of visiting. Sometimes they travel to cities, as Guarino did. Then they can check the open-air markets to see what farmers may

Did You Know?

Many drugs are made from plants. Quinine, the drug used to treat malaria, comes from the bark of the cinchona tree in South America.

Finding Lost Seeds

When Sue Osborne McBride cleaned out her freezer, she found a jar of dried beans. Not everyone gets excited when they find old beans in the freezer. But McBride was thrilled. The beans were an old variety that were named after her great aunt. They had been passed down through her family for generations. But the family had stopped growing the beans. McBride thought they were lost forever. Seeds like this are called **heirloom seeds**.

"They are no doubt over 100 years old," McBride said later. "Something like that is important to me." She planned to plant the seeds. With care and luck, they would grow. Then McBride could join the Seed Savers Exchange. Other seed savers from all around the country could trade heirloom seeds with her. Then McBride could grow other heirloom plants. She could help preserve plant diversity—in her own backyard.

have brought to town. At other times, they go to remote areas where few people live. They may have to take boats or planes to the nearest town and then hike from there.

Seed collectors go to remote places because they are looking for wild relatives of food crops. They cannot find unique wild plant seeds in a farmer's field, because most farmers plant just one species at a time. Farmers also spray their fields to prevent weeds from growing. But in remote meadows and forests, many different kinds of plants grow at once. No one sprays to kill the weeds. Seed collectors can find wild relatives of the same food plants that farmers grow in their fields.

Plant breeder Ken Street is the caretaker for a seed bank in Aleppo, Syria. He would like to find some wild rela-

Seed Savers at Home

Not all seed collectors travel to foreign countries and explore remote deserts. Some seed collectors are working to preserve crop diversity at home. Sylvia Davatz saves seeds every year in her home in Vermont. She is hoping to set up a seed-saving and seed-exchange network. She has started a business selling heirloom seeds. These seeds have been handed down in families and were bred by family farmers for generations. The seeds may not exist anywhere else in the world.

Davatz started collecting seeds when she noticed that some of her favorite foods were no longer in seed catalogs. And she found that saving seeds is easy for some foods, like beans. To save bean seeds, one just leaves the pods on the vine to dry. But saving seeds from tomatoes and beets is harder. To get seeds from a pea plant, all the gardener has to do is split open a dried pea pod and take out the peas. But to take seeds from a tomato, the gardener must carefully pick the seeds out of the wet, gooey fruit. "Some are challenging, but the more difficult it is, the more fascinating it is," Davatz says.

tives of chickpeas. Chickpeas are a type of bean. They are also called garbanzo or ceci beans. But wild chickpeas grow in places that can be dangerous to visit. One such place is southeast Turkey, next to the border with Iraq and Iran. But the danger did not stop Street from traveling there. Street has gone on seed-collecting missions through deserts and over mountain passes.

Detective Work

Seed collectors have to be part secret agent and part detective. In the 1980s, Debouck traveled through Peru and Bolivia. He was hoping to find wild giant lima beans, which are related to the smaller North American lima bean. To find them, he talked to Peruvian and Bolivian farmers about their beans. He asked them about the different kinds of beans they could remember seeing in different places. He even examined pictures of lima beans that were painted on ancient pottery. One area Debouck believed giant lima beans grew was in the Andes Mountains.

On another trip, Debouck was looking at plants in an **herbarium** in Paris, France. He found a plant that had been misplaced there. It was a bean plant that had been collected by a French explorer traveling through North America. The bean plant no longer grew in North America. Debouck took some seeds. He hopes to reintroduce the beans to the eastern United States. Debouck is also tracking some wild beans that grow only in south Florida. Those beans are safe for the moment because they grow on land that belongs to the

Due to growing concerns of extinction of native plants, a research technician gathers seeds from a cactus in San Diego, California for placement in a native seed bank.

government. Beans that grow on private land usually do not survive when cities expand or new neighborhoods are developed.

Planting Diverse Crops

Debouck, Street, Guarino, and other seed collectors are worried. They fear they do not have much time to collect unique seeds. They believe they are in a race against time. But Cary Fowler, the director of the Doomsday Vault quoted in *Popular Science* in 2008, believes that this race can be reversed. "This is the only world problem we know we can solve at this point in history," he says. "There's no clear solution for some things, like climate change . . . but for a rather limited amount of money, we can actually solve this one."

Fowler believes that the solution is to plant a greater variety of crops. Most farmers plant just one variety of each kind of crop. U.S. farmers typically grow a single type of corn on their land. But

This Iowa seed bank holds thousands of seed varieties for corn and other crops. Iowa is one of the nation's largest corn growers.

Trail of Tears Beans

Gardeners in the eastern United States have long enjoyed growing a special variety of bean, called Trail of Tears beans. During the 1830s, the United States Government forced the Cherokee and several other southeastern Native American nations to move west of the Mississippi River. The southeastern Indians did not want to leave. Soldiers forced them to march from their homes to unfamiliar lands, often at gunpoint. Their route became known as the Trail of Tears. The Cherokee, who were farmers, saved whatever seeds they could. The beans they saved and carried with them looked like small black turtle beans. Later, they became known as Trail of Tears beans.

in 1970, a corn blight hit the United States. It quickly spread through America's cornfields because each corn plant was just like every other one. Farmers watched their corn plants blacken and shrivel. The blight did not strike corn farmers in Oaxaca, Mexico nearly as hard. The Mexican farmers grow 60 different varieties of corn. So it is harder for blight to spread.

The seed vault can protect farmers from natural disasters. It gives them a place to get seeds when the crops they currently are growing fail. But Fowler hopes farmers will choose not to rely only on the seed vault. Instead, he hopes they will take action right away to protect themselves, by planting a wide variety of crop species. Farmers can create their own centers of crop diversity. Then a disaster might only harm some of a farmer's crops. The seed vault is important, and Fowler is proud of it. But he dreams of the day when it will be only a back up system.

Glossary

blight: A disease that kills an entire plant.

crop: A plant that is grown for food.

extinct: A species that no longer exists because its last members have died.

famine: A shortage of food, which causes many people to starve.

genes: Parts of cells that carry DNA, the information in cells that tells them how to grow and develop.

germinate: To sprout and begin to grow.

heirloom seeds: Seeds from plants that have been developed by local farmers or families and passed down through generations.

herbarium: A collection of plant samples.

hostages: People who have been kidnapped and held against their will, to force another person or group to take some kind of action or to pay money for their release.

plant breeders: Scientists who cross different kinds of plants together to develop a new species.

spores: A seed that a plant can make and release by itself.

variation: A plant that is a member of the same species but has genes that are a little bit different.

For More Information

Books

John Bankston, *Gregor Mendel and the Discovery of the Gene.* Hochessin, DE: Mitchell Lane, 2004. The life of plant breeder and scientist Gregor Mendel, with an explanation of his research.

Judith Jango-Cohen, *The History of Food.* New York: 21st Century Books, 2005. Covers other food-related inventions and has a chapter on genetically modified crops.

Rebecca Johnson, *Genetics*. Great Ideas of Science. Minneapolis: Lerner, 2005. Explains the science of genetics, Mendel's theories, and the discovery of DNA.

Stuart Kallen, ed. *At Issue: Is Factory Farming Harming America?* Detroit: Greenhaven Press, 2006. Provides a wide range of viewpoints related to crop diversity and genetically modified crops.

Web Sites to Visit

Julian Rubin. "Seeds and Germination: Science Fair Projects and Experiments" (www.juliantrubin.com/fairprojects/botany/seedsgermination.html). A long list of science projects related to seed germination and sprouting, with detailed instructions. Science projects are broken down by grade level.

National Gardening Association, "Finding, Gathering, Saving Seeds: Continuing the Cycle of Life" (www.kidsgardening.com/growingideas/PROJECTS/aug04/pg1.html). Explains the process of gathering and saving seeds and how kids can save seeds from their own gardens.

National Gardening Association, "When You Garden, You Grow" (www.garden.org/home). Includes a searchable directory of plants that kids can grow in their own gardens, articles about how to grow a food garden, and other how-to projects.

Index

About the Author

Bonnie Juettner is a writer and editor of children's reference books and educational videos. A former Alaskan, she is fascinated by topics related to science and the environment.